Sami's Midnight Friend

LUKE 11:5-8 FOR CHILDREN

Written by Yvonne Holloway McCall

Illustrated by Jim Roberts

Concordia Publishing House

ARCH Books

© 1971 All rights reserved.
CONCORDIA PUBLISHING HOUSE LTD.,
117/123 GOLDEN LANE, LONDON, E.C.1.
PRINTED IN ENGLAND
ISBN 0-570-06059-1

Samir slid with his bulky pack
from the woolly camel's humpy back.

He stirred the beans in his cooking pot.
"I'm starved," he cried. "I hope they're hot."

But the camel poked her nose right in
and gobbled the beans with a fiendish grin.

Samir cried,
then stopped to blink
and milked the camel
to get a drink.

But the clumsy camel kicked his hand,
and the milk was swallowed by the desert sand.

There was nothing to do.
It was time to go,
for the fiery sun
in the sky hung low.
So the caravan jolted
along its way,

and Samir went hungry the rest of the day.

The moon peeked out from behind the hill,
and Samir's tummy was empty still.
"I'm glad," thought Samir, "I have a friend
who will feed me tonight at the journey's end."

But he came to the city much too late,
and the way was blocked by a locked main gate.
So the camels were freed of their load to squeeze
through a "needle's eye" gate on bended knees.

When Samir at last saw his friend, he cried
"I feel like a hollow horn inside."
"We've nothing left," friend Benjamin said,
"but we'll go to the neighbour
and borrow some bread."
The one-room house was dark next door,
and the man inside had begun to snore.

Samir started to wail and weep,
"What can we do? He's sound asleep.
He'll never get up to give us bread
in the middle of night." But Benjamin said:

"I know he'll give us a helping hand,
for that's the custom throughout the land.
The man would be thought to be terribly rude
if he turned us away without any food."

Samir's voice grew scared and terse:
"If he *has* to answer, that's even worse.
He'll really be angry. He'll fume and roar.
He'll pound us to powder and slam the door."
But Benjamin knocked with all his might.
His deep voice shattered the quiet of night.
"I've come to borrow a bit of bread
for a hungry friend from afar," he said.

They heard the neighbour's sleepy groan,
and they knew he wished to be left alone.

But then came the sounds
of a muffled din
and the shuffle
of scuffling feet within.

"Listen," said Samir
in dread and fear,
"he's feeling around
in the dark for a spear

or a hefty hammer that weighs a ton,
and I'm much too hungry and weak to run."

Then the sound of stealthy steps was gone,
and the iron bolt on the door was drawn.
The scraping sounded throughout the house
like the screechy squeak of a giant mouse.

The children woke and wondered why,
and even the baby began to cry.

Then a burly man with weathered skin
stepped from the shadowy room within.

Samir's hands grew clammy and hot.
Was the man a friend, or was he not?

Then he thrust out his hand
without a warning.
"My wife baked this bread
early yesterday morning.

"You can see there's just enough left," he said,
"for a meal for one—three loaves of bread."
"Whew!" sighed Samir, his face aglow.
Ben said simply, "I told you so."

DEAR PARENTS:

This story is an expanded version of an illustration Jesus used to encourage His disciples to pray with confidence. Samir is a fictionalized character, but his experiences are consistent with Eastern customs and the Scripture account.

A Palestinian village of that time had no foodstores. Early in the morning the housewife would bake the day's supply of bread for the family. Three loaves were regarded as a meal for one person.

In the East it was considered a duty to entertain a guest at any time. But the neighbour could be annoyed at the disturbance. In a small, one-room house the whole family would be disturbed if the father had to get up in the night and unbolt the door.

Yet he rises and gives the man what he needs. He may not do it for the sake of friendship or because he cares but "because of his importunity." We might translate "because he is not ashamed to keep on asking." The friend inside realizes that the need must be real if it leads his friend to come at such an hour of the night and ask for food, to keep on knocking and asking until his petition is answered. The implication is that it would be unthinkable for anyone to leave his friend's request unanswered.

If this be so, then how much more will God be willing to act on our prayers! This is the point Jesus wished to make in adding this illustration when He was teaching His disciples the Lord's Prayer. And in the following verses He repeats the assurance that our heavenly Father always answers when we ask, seek, and knock in prayer.

Through faith in Jesus as our Redeemer we have a loving heavenly Father who is able and willing to hear our prayers and to act for us. You can help your child grow in this confidence.

THE EDITOR